Also by Kim Klaver (aka Ms Stud)

Book

The Truth. What it really takes to make it in Network Marketing. 1999. A 200-page full color giant cartoon book with 14 reaching out methods laid out in fun detail. 800.595.1956 or at http://www.mlm911.com

Audios

So you want to be a networker? A single audio which gives a humorous introduction to what it takes to make it in the networking business. 1996

How to Build a Giant Heap with or without your friends, family or neighbors. 2-tape set, for people doing the business. 1997

How to be an awesome sponsor and keep your heap. A single audio which shows people how to keep the ones they want to keep. 1998

Websites

http://www.maxout.com or http://www.mlm911.com
(both URL's point to the same site)
http://www.attitudestuff.com attitude wear and gear

Everything available at http://www.mlm911.com or 800.595.1956

4

Max Out Productions, Inc.
http://www.maxout.com

Virtually in every corner of the world™ ☺

Rules for
the
New

New

MLMer

Max Out Productions, Inc.
4741 Central St #300
Kansas City, MO 64112
800-595-1956
Visit our website at http://www.maxout.com

ISBN #1-891493-06-X

Klaver, Kim
Rules for the new new mlmer/Kim Klaver
Cover design:
http://www.phrizbie-design.com
and Paula English
http://www.maxout.com

Printed in the United States of America
Third Printing

Dedicated to the one who strives to think or do that thing they say cannot be done.

After all, what if it does work?™☺

"Who said it could not be done? And what great victories has he to his credit which qualify him to judge others accurately?"

Napoleon Hill

Table of Contents

0. Why this book, Rules for the New New MLMer? 10
1. What's a new new mlmer?..............................15
2. 2 rules for the new new mlmer.................. 19
3. Revolutionary belief of the new new mlmers...... 21
4. Mother Theresa Syndrome™.................... 23
5. How the airlines do it.............................. 25
6. The mission... 27
7. The Achilles' heel of the business....................29
8. 7 survival techniques............................. 32
9. The magic 1-4...................................... 34
10. How do your prospects rate?.................... 38
11. How fast will they go?............................ 42
12. The 5 worst things you can say... 45
13. The question that's the answer.................... 57
14. No more pretending you love 'no'............... 60
15. Stop doing things you hate in new new mlm... 62
16. To use or not to use the 'mlm' word?........... 65
17. The art of network conversation-1
     How do I know the product will work?............ 68
18. The art of network conversation-2
     "How do I know the business will work?"........ 70
19. The art of network conversation-3
     "Well I'd like to try the business..." 72
20. The art of network conversation-4
     "Should I send them a package? Costs $!"...... 74
21. The art of network conversation-5
     "What about flaky do-nothing downline?"............76

22. The art of network conversation-6
    "My good prospect is stalling. What can I do?"...... 78
23. The art of network conversation-7
    "What if they ask: Is this a pyramid? MLM?"...... 80
24. Narrow the focus, get the attention
    What an airline did
25. Cher's advice for anyone you're dragging 84
26. How to tell if the advice is any good or not 85
27. How to tell if your pitch is any good or not 87
28. The doctor is 'in'
    "What should I say when they call?" 90
29. How to drastically improve your odds 94
30. Reducing the effect of the dud factor 96
31. Goodbye message 98
32. Say 'no' first 100
33. Quick way to 'web-ify yourself' 105
34. "The Internet is the greatest direct marketing
    medium ever invented." 106
35. Target the right customers online 108
36. Finding people online who want what you have ... 109
37. How to create effective email messages,
    with permission 112
38. Romancing your prospects 116
39 What should you say to your 'target' audience? ... 120
40. Say it with a signature 124
41. For writers 126
42. So now what? 128
☺ Abbreviated bibliography 130

Why this book, '**R**ules for the New New MLMer'?

Over the last four years, I've been hosting international conference calls once or twice a week. Reps from 300+ companies have been on those calls. 30-40 companies are typically represented on each call.

These phone get-togethers are designed to entertain, motivate and keep networkers in the business long enough to land a 'right' one, somewhere in their organization, in their lifetime.

Following the Chicago 'big 6' of the early 1900s*, I almost always begin each call with this question:

What obstacles, if you could overcome them, would move your business ahead the most?

* The Chicago 'big 6' included Wm. Wrigley Jr., founder of the chewing gum empire, Messrs. Ritchie and Hertz, owners of the Yellow taxicab business, and 4 other well known Chicagoans, each of whom built their empires from zip, and with no special education. The 6 attributed their phenomenal success to their regular weekly mastermind meetings. See Law of Success, N Hill p. 75

Here are the obstacles that have been offered most often:

Finding good people
Getting good people to listen to the opportunity
Keeping your people motivated
Keeping yourself motivated

Getting good people to see the big picture
Overcoming objections
Unsupportive, even pukey family and friends
Not enough money to do it
Broke people

They agree but don't do anything
Not enough time to do it
Don't know, what, exactly, to do anyway
Don't know how to prioritize my time
Have only do-nothing downline

Never knew how many pukies were out there
Never really knew my 'friends' were just talkers
No one calls me back anymore
My upline can sell product, but doesn't know how to do the business building part...so can't teach me

No upline support
Can't stand my upline
Home office not responsive-plus nobody there's ever done it before
Etc. etc. etc.

By the way, all companies' reps have these problems. Reps from these companies have reported them on the calls:

(And of course those from many companies that are no longer with us, e.g. Int'l Heritage, Jewelway, Destiny, STS)

ACN Inc.
Alpine Industries
Amazon Herb Company
Amway
Arbonne Intl
Big Planet
Body Systems Intl
Body Wise
CellTech
Changes Intl
Discovery Toys
Enrich
EOLA Int'l
Essential Oils
Essentially Yours
Industries
Excel Communications
FlashNet
Communications
ForMor
Freelife
FreeNet
Herbal Life
Heritage Health
Idea Concepts

IDN
I-Link
Kaire Intl
km.net
Legacy
Life Plus
Life Force Int'l
Life Science
Longevity
Mannatech
Market America
Mary Kay
Melaleuca
Morinda
MultiPure
New Image
New Vision
Neways
Nikken
NSA
NuSkin
Nutrition for Life
NutrQuest
Optimal Telecom
Oxyfresh

Pampered Chef   Royal Body Care
PPL   Shaklee
Preferred Price Plus   Shaperight
Primerica   SkyBiz 2000
ProStep   TravelMax
Renaissance for Life   Usana
Rexall Showcase
Vision Quest
Watkins
Young Living

The Surprise

After hearing this litany of difficulties from each other and all the different companies, everybody 'fesses up each time that they had NO IDEA this is what it would really be like.

And, participants added, had they known it would be like this, they would have wanted some real scrimmage-like training. Like boot camp for the Marines or the Army, where you get to practice doing stuff so you get really good before you're sent out to do the real thing.

The purpose of this little volume is to give you the rules for doing just that...in this new age of network marketing, or mlm (**m**ulti **l**evel **m**arketing) as it is known among many. Revolutionary rules for the new new mlm as practiced by the new new mlmers. Ready? Here goes...☺

14

BLANK PAGE

1
What's a new new mlmer?

Over the last 50 years, the great majority of the millions
introduced to mlm didn't make it.

Did you know that?

They never got what they were seeking with the business.
So they quit, and became a statistic. A talking statistic,
however, with a bad taste in her mouth. A statistic that
lives on to tell others about her unhappy experience(s).

Most of those moms, dads, college students and elderlies
who gave out were never given an honest chance to make it
to begin with. Because nobody told them the truth about
what it takes to make it.

This is not a good thing. For five decades, those poor old
mlmers-to-be went in with their eyes wide shut, as it were.
They were totally unprepared for what was about to happen
to them.

Those were the days of the old mlmers.

The astonishing failure rate of the past is one reason the whole industry has (had) such a black eye. The other shame is that in the face of this incredible failure rate, so many 'leaders' continue to talk, no, *scream*, the hype about, uh, well, you know. That:

1. It's easy. Anyone can do it.

2. You can/will make [insert big, impressive number here suitable for the listener] almost immediately in this business

3. 'Everyone' will want this product/service

12. Our [deal/company/pay plan/ management team] is the best [in the history of the world/ out there].

5.   All you have to do is talk to people you know.

Now I ask you: Why would anyone keep saying that stuff when the truth is known to anyone with experience, especially 'leaders' in front of the room?

We call these 'The 5 worst things you can say to a good prospect." They're discussed on pp. 45-56)

Surely people whose brains are set to 'on' know better than 'the 5 worst things,' don't we?

Was that a 'yes'? Well then, welcome to the ranks of the new new mlmers!

'New' if you know these things and just started a program for the first time ever, and new new if you know this and are starting your first 90 days over again.

This little volume is for you, the new new mlmer.

People who believe these truths with us, and who now want new, better rules of conduct. Rules that work for the majority instead of just a teensie, weensie minority.

P.S. For you surprised, experienced mlmers, we'll grant that maybe, once upon a time, the 'the 5 worst things,' might have been true for a select few. Perhaps you were among them.

But in the new millennium, 'the 5 worst things…' have become an albatross for the average person starting out in the business. Deceptive but alluring, 'the 5 worst…' continue to be hyped in meetings, phone conference calls, online through endless emails, and in one-on-ones by the non-thinking mlmers.

The '5 worst...' are perhaps the #1 cause of the miserable and unhappy results so many people have experienced.

And, the continued trumpeting of the '5 worst...' is probably responsible for the perception out there that the business is something only low enders would, could or should do.

So, what's an old mlmer? Someone who continues telling the '5 worst things...' to new recruits and those who are trying and stumbling,

What's a new new mlmer? Someone who knows better than the '5 worst things...' and who now wants new, better and more honest things to say.

Let 2000 mark the end of the outdated, outworn ways. Let it mark the beginning of the way of the new new mlm and its new practitioners, the new new mlmers.

What do you think? Shall we?

2

2 rules for the new new mlmer

Rule 1. Stay away from people who try to recruit you by telling you any of 'the'5 worst things...' [see pp. 45-56] or some other cliched pitch. Immediately find another, smarter, more honest and sensible sponsor.

Here's how to tell if *any* 'pitch' line/header is worth your precious time or not.

Start with one of 'the 5 worst' or any other pitch line. Repeat the words of the pitch line slowly, with the TV, CD, or radio turned off. Then ask yourself 5 questions about that pitch line. Let's try it with worst thing #1.

'It's easy. Anyone can do it.'

The 5 questions to ask:

Does this sound really credible to me?
Who is telling me this? What do I know about them?
How do they know this?
How can I come to know if this is credible or not?
Given all this, do I want to pursue this now or not?

Of course, make certain that whatever pitch line you use can withstand the same test.

Rule **2.** Do not ruin your chances of landing a good prospect by allowing yourself to parrot any of the '5 worst' cliches. Turn on your personal voice monitor to clear your throat of these 5 worst things…' [pp. 45-56] before they come out of your mouth.

3
Revolutionary belief of the new new mlmers

Here's a revolutionary belief for the new new mlmer:

Most important is the survival of #1. It is everything
and the only thing in the beginning. Without #1,
there can be no #2, #3...

Most people say they are in mlm because they had a life
changing experience and want to offer it to others. Like
religion, kind of. People enjoy spreading things around
that work for them. And it's great to get paid for it as well,
here on earth. Paid to help others, that is.

Unbeknownst to these innocent beginners, however, is this:
The biggest trick in the business of network marketing is
surviving the hazards of telling and sharing at all. Like
Jesus' disciples then and now, to carry on, one must survive
the emotionally perilous process of spreading the word, and
the fallout from family and friends from the doing of it.
Especially when seeking converts. Others just don't
always respond in the way you might expect.

Chances of survival can be dramatically increased if
someone prepares you for the harsh realities of what's to
come. But because the truth about the journey has been
kept hidden from new recruits in the past, no one thought
there was much to get ready for. Just start talking and
that's that. Ha.

Once the perils of the undertaking are presented (along with the prize, of course), preparation for survival becomes the clear first step.

So first off, **install the revolutionary belief.**

> Most important is the survival of #1. It is everything and the only thing in the beginning. Without #1, there can be no #2, #3...

Once the onslaught starts from the naysayers and pukeys, falling back on the *revolutionary belief* is what will help save the new recruits.

You remember though, that knowing X and doing X are not the same, yes? (Where would diet consultants be if people actually did what they knew?)

So, once this *revolutionary belief* is firmly installed in the bone marrow, new recruits will ask for some basic survival techniques before they start out. You can now offer 7 of them to motivated-to-learn-them recruits. (See pp. 32-33)

4
Mother Theresa Syndrome™

Perhaps the biggest impediment to installing the
revolutionary belief is 'Mother Theresa Syndrome™
(MTS). That's this:

Mother Theresa Syndrome™   When you want it more for them than they want it for themselves.

Because so many people in network marketing say they're
in it because they *did* have a life changing experience (kind
of like religion), the urge to 'save the world' quite naturally
takes over. Everyone with X problem can now be saved
(because I was), and I'm saving them now!

Whether they want to be saved or not...
Whether they asked for help or not...
Whether they 'see it' or not
Whether they respond or not...

The modus operandi when one has full on MTS is "I'm
gonna MAKE you do it. I have to bang on you till you say
yes because you need this. Because I care about you and I
really want to save you from [whatever]."

I daresay the loudest wail throughout mlm land is: *Can't
we just make them do it? How can I make X see this?*

The effect of Mother Theresa Syndrome™? Mostly gloom
on the mlmer who, crusading from an honest, helpful heart,
does not understand why the rest of the world, especially
people they know, just refuse to be saved. At least not now,
when the mlmer needs it most.

Too many people in the industry have 'died' trying to
save others, especially early in their careers. Not a good
thing.

So how can we redirect this urge? So it doesn't cost a well-
meaning person their career in the new new mlm?

Two things. First, study what others do, like the airlines, to
save good people from this kind of fatal mistake (next).
Second, learn 7 survival tricks to save yourself for the right
ones (pp. 32-33).

5
How the airlines do it

One place where the survival of #1 is given highest priority, with everyone's wholehearted consent, is on a commercial airliner. Airline personnel are taught that the human tendency is to, well, here's what the airlines do.

On every flight. Every time. Before take off.

"Ladies and gentlemen: In case of sudden loss of air pressure, the oxygen masks will drop from the ceiling. Put your own mask on first, and then help children and people acting like children."

Have you ever noticed that's what they say, every single time?

Why do you think they say that?

How much can you help someone else if you're not able to function yourself, i.e. if you are losing consciousness?

Network marketing for the new new mlmer is the same. You MUST take care of #1. That means, before you start looking for people to help, make sure you are capable of helping yourself first. Have your 'attitude oxygen mask' ready so that whenever the going gets tough, you can help yourself survive, AND be able to help others.

Without attitude-oxygen, your drive will fade. Then you run the risk of acute attitude failure. This is not a good thing. How can you help others then? Or yourself? ☹

So first and foremost, don your attitude-oxygen mask. Whatever it takes, to keep YOUR attitude right. Keep reading. We've got some suggestions. ☺

6
The mission

Let's agree on the mission for you, your new recruits and anyone else who wants to be a new new mlmer.

Mission: Find people for whom it's the right thing to be doing now. No one else.

Anyone not agree with that?

Anyone want to keep recruiting people for whom it's not the right thing to be doing now?

OK. That means, then, no more recruiting anyone you have to drag across the finish line. It is OK to let go of those you are dragging. Now is good.

Pushing the wrong ones to sign can be extremely stressful. Even damaging. Many people have come to regret ever having signed up certain people.

Here's what some 'wrong ones' did to a bank:

In her book, *Customers.com*, Seybold writes about a bank, which had just discovered by detailed analysis that "20% of its customers were responsible for 100% of the profits." Sound familiar? It gets worse:

"...The 80% left eroded it (the bank's profit) down to what appears on the bank's income statement."

Bummer, huh? So what should you do with the 80% 'wrong customers' who 'eroded the bank's profit' down and down?   And were responsible for $0 of the bank's profit?

Well, Seybold reports that she recommended this to the bank:

Do whatever it takes to "encourage the wrong customers to defect...to someone else" for whom they might be a better match. Yeah. Let someone else have people who are losers and drags on you. ☺

7
The Achilles' heel of the business

You know the mission: **Find people for whom it's the right thing to be doing now. No one else.**

Of course, this is easier said than done.

Here's why: Remember how James Bond (007) gets outfitted before he takes off? He has every new and cool gadget on his person and in his car, so he'll be ready to respond to the perils he and the outfitters are expecting him to run into. You know, en route to accomplishing the big mission, right? Plus he receives hands on training in the use of all gizmos.

The new new mlmer also has some obstacles to overcome. Here's a biggie:

90%+ of people they will interact with, SAY they want what you offer. I.e. more income, more energy, better health, fewer aches and pains, a web presence, less expensive long distance, more money left at the end of the month, etc. Sounds good, they say. Great!

BUT, uh…
of those *say 'Yes's'* how many would you bet are willing to make a change to get what they just said they want?

We defer to anyone with ANY experience: think back to
just last week. How many was it? Maybe 2%-10%?
That's the answer we got on everyone of our hundreds of
national conference calls.

This unbelievable discrepancy is the Achilles' heel of the
industry:

Achilles' heel of the industry
For every 20 people you talk to who will **say**
'yes, I want that now,' just 1 or 2 will actually **do** 'yes.'

---

19 of the 20 are just talking, complaining, whining, tire
kicking, or too tired. Not ready to make a change now.
And that's ok.

Except no one said this might happen. That's why no one
gets ready and, well, you know, they end up like Achilles.
'Shot' in the weak spot no one told them about. ☹

(Remember how Achilles believed he was invincible? And
he was, except in the one spot on his heel where his mother
had held on to him as a baby, when dunking him into the
magic waters that protected the rest of him. That heel was
his weak spot, but he didn't know it. Until it was too late,
of course, and an arrow sped directly to the spot).

So now what?

Since you now know this miserable little secret, you can prepare for it, unlike Achilles. He died because he didn't know. Just like the old mlmers. ☹

This fate need not befall you. Because now you know. ☺

8
7 Survival techniques

1. Know the *Mission* and teach it to all new recruits and faltering oldies:

Mission: Find people for whom it's the right thing to be doing now. No one else.

2. Get the *revolutionary belief* into your bone marrow

Revolutionary belief
Most important is the survival of #1. It is everything and the only thing in the beginning. Without #1, there can be no #2, #3...

3. Prepare for the Achilles' heel of the business:

Achilles' heel of the business
For every 20 people you talk to who will **say** 'yes, I want that now,' just 1 or 2 will actually **do** 'yes.'

4. Learn to say 'No' first (pp. 100-104).

5. Always have 3-5 ROMS (Reaching Out Methods) going on to hedge your bets and keep it interesting (pp. 94-95).

6. Do all ROMS (Reaching Out Methods) in teams to prevent painful fallout (pp. 96-97).

7. Laugh and breathe deeply at least 3 times each day.

9
The magic 1-4

QUESTION: How many people does it really take for those top network marketers to make that $10,000 to $100,000+ per MONTH?

Well, would you believe:

The top bananas in the major network marketing companies have 1 to 4 people who generate 80-90% of ALL that income.

This includes the really big bananas who make $100k+ per month!

Even more astonishing, most of them have ONE person whose organization is responsible for near 50% or more of their total income.

And as often as not, that one person isn't even front-line to the big gun! But signed up by someone else, lower down, who didn't even know the great one on top.

How did we find out?

We asked.

Admissions of the great ones

(Interview with Top 10 Presidential Directors Randy and Melissa Davis, Excel Communications. $1million dollar a year earners. They've been with the company 7 years, and are independent reps.)

Interviewer: Kim Klaver, AKA Ms. Stud

Ms. Stud: So, my successful friends, how many people did you sponsor front line (=personally sign up)?

Randy: About 110, maybe 120.

Ms. Stud: And umm, how many of those flaked?

Melissa: Uhh, all but about 10. We have 10 active lines -- people we personally sponsored who sponsored others.

(Quick quiz: OK. How many flaked? And what percent is that of the total they personally signed up?)

Ms. Stud: So, how many people in your entire organization does it take to give you, say 80% of your income?

Randy: Well, uhh...

Melissa: Honey, I think it's just two, isn't it?

Randy: Yup, two key people provide 80% or more of our income. That's right.

Ms. Stud: So how did you get your two 'studs of the earth', as we say around here?

Randy: (straining) Well, we sponsored the mechanic, right?

Melissa: (eyes rolled heavenward) Yeah, and he--uhh--sponsored...and then they sponsored, umm, actually, the stud in that line is underneath three, no, he's FOUR down.

Ms. Stud: Did you know him before? Is that how you got him?

Randy: Oh yeah! We knew him!

Melissa: But we didn't personally recruit him, did we dear?

Randy: We sure didn't. But I'm glad he's a super stud, aren't you?

Ms. Stud: And what about the other one? Don't hold back...tell all!

Randy: (shyly) Actually, we didn't personally recruit him, either.

Ms. Stud: How far down is he?

Randy: What do you think, honey?

Melissa: He's 8 deep

Ms. Stud: So, two key people, one 4 down, and one 8 down, are responsible for more than 80% of your income, yes? Oh, did you know #8?

Randy: Nope. We do now, though. And are we ever glad and thankful!

From *The Truth...What it really takes to make it in Network Marketing.*

Moral: Nobody needs many key people to make the big income. You don't even need to know a great one yourself. You've just got to stick around long enough so you or someone in your organization gets a good one. Just like Randy and Melissa have done and continue to do.

"Remember Jesus only had 12 and now look! One quarter of the world's population is in his organization."
(*So You Want to be a Networker* audio)

Who else is at the top with the magic 1-4? Jordan Adler, *Excel*; Jackie Blasko, *Market America*; Jeff&Carla Breakey, *Life Force*; David & Colli Butler, *FreeLife;* Michael Clutton, *Evision;* Ray Gebauer, *Mannatech*; Sarah Guetshow, *Tax People*; Dave & Coni Johnson, *NuSkin*; Dave Johnson, *Nikken;* Usa Johnson, *Morinda*; Donna Larson-Johnson, *Arbonne;* Brenda & Jerry Loffredo, *PPL*; Judy Marshall, *KingsWay* ; David Mitchell, *Designer Technologies*; David Nelson, *ForMor*; Karl & Fern Prazak, *E'OLA*; Becca Rae, *ProStep*; Ira Spector, *Royal Body Care*; Todd Smith, *American Longevity*; Diane Walker/Jack Bastide, *Heritage Health*, Larry & Bev Williams, *Rexall Showcase;* Rick Wolter, *Herbalife Life*, to name a few.

38

10
How do your prospects rate?

How can you tell which of your prospects is likely to be one of the magic 1-4?

Here's a quick way to check and see how a prospect stacks up.

Run them through the 'Prospect Scale.' Here it is:

---

1   2   3   4   5   6   7   8   9   10

1-3s are people whose working background is/was exclusively as an employee for someone else. The numbers distinguish quality of performance. So 1 is not so good, 3 is stellar.

The slow, sullen employee at the restaurant is a 1.

The one who's friendly and goes 'the extra mile' for you is a 3.

4-6s represent people who own their own business. From the one person show to one with employees. Franchise owners come in here, too. Anyone on 100% commission is also a 4-6, e.g. real estate brokers/agents or any other direct sales people (Kirby or Electrolux vacuum cleaners, Fuller Brush, etc.). Anyone whose income depends solely on their own performance. 4s are not too good at it. 6s are great.

7-10s are people with some to lots of network marketing experience. 7s not so successful, 10s are the ones everyone dreams of at night.

What you should know about them...

Employee. Gets a fixed, guaranteed 'salary'. Should an employee need supplies, they go directly to the supply cabinet and take whatever they need. Nothing to buy for doing their job. Pencils and sharpeners provided and available.

Employees are the ones who might ask the dreaded question:

"What??? You mean I have to spend my own money to do this?!?"

Now you know why. That might take out some of the sting.

Fear of employee: What's the guaranteed income?

Business/franchise owner/100% commission sales.
Buys own pencils and pencil sharpeners. So they
understand laying out of money and effort to build a
business.

Big daily fear of business owners: That his/her agents or
employees will leave and start their own competing
business 'across the street'. So the best training tips they
know are kept secret.

Business owners' need in networking Must come to trust
sharing his/her best ideas with the new recruits. "Why?"
he asks? Here's why: So the new recruits succeed and
throw off some income to him/her, enabling the business
owner to work a little less. Oh. Why didn't you say so?

Networker. Already buys own pencils AND Kleenex.

Networkers' need: To discover that there are good
alternatives to contacting friends, family and neighbors.
Because they'll have burned through most of them in
prior deals that went belly-up.

The big question to get the Prospect Scale information.

Let's say someone's calling you because they read or heard
info about what you market, and they're calling to get more
information. Before you launch into your pitch, go into the
doctor mode (pp. 90-93) and ask the introductory question:

"Glad you called. So, what attracted you to this, given the information you read/heard so far?"

(You'll know what they seek right off and you can decide whether what you have is right for them or not.)

Whatever they say, assuming they have life force and you're still interested, here's the big question to place them somewhere on the Prospect Scale immediately:

> "Great. So let me ask you, have you ever done anything like this before? Direct sales, or network marketing? Or have you ever owned your own business?"

The response to this one question will tell you their professional background as it relates to the Prospect Scale.

Then you can reasonably guesstimate how long it will take for them to get up to speed on what it takes to build a successful networking business. This will help you decide with whom to spend the most time first. And whom you might pass down to others in your organization. ☺

11
How fast will they go?
3 Questions to get at how fast and when

When someone expresses an interest, then what? How do you get them off the pot?

Here's how to find out immediately how ready, willing and able they are to go, now. Plus, how to get a time commitment and spending plan for the first 6 months.

Three 'knock 'em off the fence' questions will do it. (from the Truth book p. 192)

The 3 questions fit right into a typical scenario: a prospect is ready to learn about doing the business, and asks:

THEM: Well, what does one actually do to build a successful networking business?

YOU: OK. Here's what we do: We reach out in lots of ways to find people who'd like to get the same kinds of benefits we get, right? That's what we do to grow our business. You got that part, right?

THEM. Yesss, but I'm not sure how...

YOU: Well, there are lots of ways to reach out. To people you know and people you don't know. There are ways to make people come to you and ways where you go first.

Ways that cost money and ways that don't. So, you tell me which you want to see first, and I'll show you what we do.

Then, whatever you want to try, you can watch a team that's doing that thing, either in person or over the phone. And after you watch other people doing it, you can try it. Think you could do that?

THEM: Sure.

YOU: Great. So let me ask you this: How fast do you want to go? Turbo speed, medium, or the leisure track?

THEM: Turbo (or other choice)

YOU: Great. How much time and money can you commit to building your business in the first six months, whether you make any money or not during that time? Pick a number between say, $50 and $500/mo, or more, you know, for business cards and reaching out. Tell me what you can do, so I can help you get the most bang for your buck and for the time you can commit.

THEM: Pick the time and $

YOU: So when are you ready to get started?

THEM: Pick date and time ☺ or, they flake ☹.

Set up a schedule now with ones ready to go. Get them signed in, start them on the product or program, and schedule the times when the reaching out will begin *with others*. Do not delay here, or their interest will wane. Set it up now and follow up.

New new mlmers do not expect new recruits to do this alone. You'll likely have a dead recruit within a week if you do, just like old mlmers ☹.

Remember, reaching out to find new people is the most treacherous part of the business. Let NO ONE do that alone. Being alone and hearing that unexpected 'no' or worse is the #1 reason new people drop out the weekend after they've signed up. This is the time to be with others on the same track.

Just like the teams that climb Mt. Everest. They're all tied together with rope. Just in case someone (expert climbers all) slips. Who do you think holds them up? Uh huh. This is the same. ☺

12

The 5 Worst Things you can say to a good prospect

(Reprinted from http://www.mlm911.com)

Each week on our big national conference calls, people from the 35-45 companies on the line tell us their biggest obstacle to success is this:

Finding good people to talk to and, when they finally have one, getting that person to even LISTEN to the opportunity.

Everybody seeks those elusive, good people.

The kind who are committed to do what it takes to make it. Obsessed. Resilient. Ambitious. Not easily influenced by others once they've made up their own minds, based on their own research and personal experiences. Fun people. Friendly, open-minded people. Self-starters. Hard working. Will do whatEVER it takes. And of course, they will have a major sphere of influence over other people just like them. Yes.

Shall we agree that this is a likely definition of a 'good person' for the business? Oh, and they're definitely not whiney or pukey towards new ideas and new things.

Let's say we agree who the 'good people' are. Did you realize the things they usually teach you to say from the front of the room typically turn these kinds of people right off? Oiy vey! Really?

Everybody knows that step one is attracting good people, and then, getting them to listen, yes?

Well, for good people like this, of whom I consider myself one, and I believe many of my readers consider themselves ones too, here are the 5 worst things you can say to any of us:

1. "It's easy. Anyone can do it."

Why would anyone tell a good, new prospect this? If it were really true, why do 90% plus of the people who sign up, cave?

Besides, whom do you actually attract when you say that? What do people who hear that expect they have to do to make it in the business?

While it may be true that cerebral brain power is not what one needs to make it big in networking, shouldn't we stop pretending that it's easy and anyone can do it? Otherwise, wouldn't EVERYONE be making it?

The second worst thing you can say to a good prospect is:

2. "You can/will make [big money/a fortune/$10k+/mo] almost immediately in this business."

Predicting the future like this for someone else is pure hype. Be it about the product ('you will lose X lbs./you will feel like new', etc) the potential income, or how others will feel about it ('You'll love it!' 'Your friends will love it!')

Hype is easily recognizable to anyone with brains, and even people with not so much grey matter.

First, be honest with yourself: how often does that big income happen right away, or even ever, for most people? If it's so easy, how come so many people don't make it?

Good people don't fall for this nonsense. But guess who does? Yes. Sorry. It's those people who want something for nothing or next to nothing. Yahoo's Seth Godin calls them the *"dreaded opportunity seekers...someone with more time than money, a nonconsumer who focuses on low-margin items and is a less than ideal prospect for most products."* (Permission Marketing, P.108)

Is that who you want on your team? Well then, please stop asking for them.

The third worst thing you can say to a good prospect is:

3. "'Everyone' will want this product/service"

While maybe true theoretically, this is what almost every network marketing company says about its services and product lines. In fact, it's what most every company out there say about their wares.

Picture this: New people going off, after the 'meeting' thinking that 'everyone' will want this, or that the stuff/service is for 'everyone.' What happens when they go home and call a few people and hear the usual 'it's too expensive' and 'I can't believe you fell for that' types of responses?

Uh huh. They figure, either the people in the front were lying or, worse, 'I'm not smart enough to do this, I guess. Better give the stuff back.' And after the first few calls, it's over.

This doesn't mean the products or services COULD not be beneficial to the whole world. But does that mean that everyone WILL do the thing? Or will love it like you do?

You may believe in your heart of hearts that everyone SHOULD do 'it' (=whatever you're selling that you believe in) or use it, or whatever, but doesn't McDonald's marketing team think the same thing? Or people who make Hondas?

They can't figure it out either. Why doesn't EVERYONE
eat at McDonalds? Why doesn't EVERYONE drive a
Honda? Or eat Snickers? Or buy Crest toothpaste? Or eat
organically grown food? Or exercise when they know they
should?

What's wrong with all these people out there, anyway?

Smart marketing people are finally beginning to 'target'
their potential users ('target marketing') so they direct their
spiel at the ones for whom it's the right thing to be using.
(E.g. our products are for people who are 'adventuresome'
or who 'put family first,' etc). A tiny fraction of the total
people out there. But it works much better. They get
the right ones AND those who wish they could be
(or perceived to be) 'adventuresome' or 'intelligent'.

In the network marketing world, the 'right ones' are people
with some entrepreneurial flair and readiness to change.
 2-10% of people out there, it is said, over and over, by
those in the trenches.

What fools everyone is this: nearly everybody we know
SAYS they want more freedom, more income, more
energy, residual income, more blah blah blah.

**But what percent of those same people are willing to
make a change and do something about it?**

A paltry 3-10%. There's the rub. Everyone who's ever lived a day in the life of a networker has experienced it.

So, could your 'thing' be helpful and beneficial to everyone? Maybe. Will everyone 'see it' or do it?

Complaining about a thing and doing something about that thing are well, not the same. There's maybe 1 doer for every 20 complainers and wannabes. The rest are just venting, a very in thing these days. If in doubt, ask:

"Do you really want [THE BENEFIT] or are you just venting?"

And there's your answer. Accept it, and act accordingly. Venting is not a crime. I mean, doesn't everyone just 'vent' once in a while? You just need to know that's what they're doing, that's all. So ask.

P.S. In 'THE BENEFIT' blank, insert *that extra income, more free time, residual income, your own money, more energy, tax savings, legal protection, an internet business, a new life* or whatever they said 'attracted' them to the business in the first place.

The fourth worst thing you can say to a good prospect is:

4. "Ours (this) is the best [deal/company/pay plan/management (you name it)] in the history of the world/out there."

To utter these words with any credibility, shouldn't the speaker have personally done EVERY deal, been in every company, tried every product, or met and worked with every management team out there? How else could anyone even offer an opinion like this?

How many who say this do you think are qualified to say it?

Actually, isn't #4 just a silly thing to say? That is what EVERY company says about themselves. And what would you expect them to say?

Who cares? (Saying something different than #4 has wonderful consequences. Think Avis, whose slogan 'we try harder' because they're #2 has made them a household name. America has been in love with the underdog forever.)

Even when people **do** try the very same things, they have different reactions, don't they?

Say 3 people try 5 different hamburger joints. Chances are that each of them would give a different opinion as to which is their first choice.

Depends on your tastes, yes?

Is anything 'best' for everyone?

Experience tells us something else. For example, Rolls Royces are for people with money, who enjoy showing it. Not ALL people with money, but those (of them) that like to show it. Sam Walton, the richest guy in the world in his day (not long ago), drove a 10-year-old truck even when he was, when he drove it, the richest man in the world (according to *Fortune* magazine).

So even just here, within this single elite class of the very rich, we observe differences in preference. Nothing is 'best' for everyone. No one would want that except the owners of the supposed 'best thing' or 'best belief' or 'best way.'

'Best in the world' for everyone is the same thing religious zealots preach.

They too, say their 'deal' is the best in the history of the world. But isn't it based mostly on faith? A very strong feeling of certainty someone has? And doesn't a person's faith depend largely on where they live? And how and where they were brought up? And to whom they have been exposed in life? And what's happened to them?

Think Bombay, versus Rome, or the Midwest or Iraq.
Very different beliefs, yes? Not very conducive to a 'one
for all' mentality. Plus, who wants to change their own
beliefs? Everyone wants the other to change theirs.

And the zealots really try to make that happen. Remember
the religious crusades? It is reported that religious wars are
the #1 cause of death and destruction in the history of
civilization. And what are those wars based on? The
insistence by one group or another that THEIR DEAL is
the best for EVERYONE and, if you don't agree, well then
we'll just have to crush you. And they have, and they still
do. Almost no religious group is exempt from this
intolerance. Insistence on 'my one best belief system or
else' still justifies killing and cruelty all over the world, by
otherwise normal and good people.

But some leaders are coming around to a more tolerant and
open-minded perspective. Did you know what the Pope did
in March, 2000? For the first time in the history of the
Church, he offered an official, public apology for the
Church's participation in the crusades of yesteryear. That
was when, in the name of the Church, members cruelly
tormented and erased any and all 'non-believers in
'our best way' (including women and children).

The people you want to attract know better than to buy the
line *Ours (this) is the best deal/company/pay
plan/management (you name it) in the history of the world,
for you and everyone in the world* just because someone
else says it or believes it.

54

People prefer choice. And choice is what they will have or create, depending on who they are and what they think is important.

Surprisingly, when marketing anything, the more narrow, specific and *limiting* your stated audience is, the more people seem to flock to it. Think Harvard. Thousands of applications for each student admitted. Now, how would you market Harvard? A place for people who...? You fill it in. Would it be for 'everyone' or just people who blah and blah and probably blah blah and then some more blahs?

Same here. "X is for people who..." and the more narrow and specific that is, the better it attracts those people and hoards of others who won't even qualify, but who can't resist. Like applying to Harvard. Besides, they may know people.

The 5th worst thing you can say to a good prospect is:

5. "All you have to do is talk to people you know."

Telling new people this is worst of all. And not just because it isn't true. (Unless you are President or some famous deity who can actually influence others to at least try the thing being sold, like celebrities who endorse products and companies.) It's because this one fib is the #1 reason new people don't make it. You know it, don't you? Picture it. Re-experience it...

There goes an innocent new baby in the business, happily off to talk to people they know, expecting to sign them up and sell them the dream or save them. Without one ounce of preparation for what they're in for. And after the first few calls, it's usually over, or nearly over.

Who would have thought what misery friends and family wreak on an innocent new person? The worst pukies are friends and family. And it doesn't take many of these reactions. 3-10, usually, before the new baby is out of the game ☹.

Going to friends and family right off should be outlawed, so new people at least have a chance to make it. AFTER they've had some success, perhaps they can entertain the idea.

Instead of risking approaching friends, people can send a Dear Friend Letter (in Truth book). It removes the risk of getting dumped on. Because only the ones who have an interest call back. So no one even hears 'no.' ☺

Think of the hours on the phone chatting about hemorrhoids or failed marriages that they get to skip.

Everyone knows about Napoleon Hill, yes? He wrote *Think and Grow Rich*, perhaps the best known book in the English speaking world after the Bible. Nearly every industry leader claims they've read it. They recommend it to anyone and everyone. But they don't follow his advice.

It is Mr. Hill who said that perhaps the biggest reason people fail in life is the tendency to listen to friends, family and neighbors. In his own words:

"Close friends and relatives...often handicap one through 'opinions' and...ridicule...meant to be humorous. Thousands of men and women carry inferiority complexes with them all through life, because some well-meaning but ignorant person destroyed their confidence through 'opinions' or ridicule."

Think and Grow Rich p 140-141.

This, after 20 years of full time research asking what it takes to be successful in life. Walking and talking with the likes of Thomas Edison, John Rockefeller and Andrew Carnegie and 497 other self-made men.

And they want you to send a good new recruit into this destructive environment without preparation? ☹

New new mlmers will offer lots of alternatives to finding good people, like the 14 methods of reaching out described in the Truth book and Giant Heap tapes (see pp. 94-95 for some). Really.

Besides, in what start up business does anyone ever say 'all you have to do is go talk to people you know' to make it big? Good people expect there to be more to it than that. And we all know there is, don't we? ☺

13
The question that's the answer

Many potential recruits ask shortsighted questions, and by doing so, tell you what kind of protégé they will be. Can you ask a 'wrong' question? Yes! A question tells what one seeks, and what that person is seeking may not be creating a successful business, but a quick score, or an excuse to pass. Better to know up front, yes? For example:

How fast can I make $$$?

How much does it cost to do this?

Someone asking these questions may not have the attitude it takes to build a successful business. Any business.

Here is a better question:

What does it take to build a successful business?

You already know about the 'wrong ones' who are not ready to make a change now. Those were the easy ones.

People who pass that first test, but who do not realize or will not accept that building a successful business requires a commitment that goes beyond just signing up, are not right ones, either. They're a little more tricky. Because they sound hopeful at first.

58

Starting a business is something like having a baby. How much does it cost to have a baby? Well, the delivery cost of that baby isn't nearly as much as the cost of the commitment required to care for, nourish, support and love it over the years it takes to grow up. Every parent has learned that. Much to the surprise of some.

Are you willing to commit to the care and feeding of your business?

Do you want people who feel the same?

Tidbits

Mae West
According to a recent issue of New Yorker magazine, Mae West "...never doubted her stardom, though it took her thirty years to make the world agree." What about you? Is it worth it to keep caring for and feeding your business, even if you don't know how long it will take for the world 'to agree' and just 'give' it to you? Like it did Mae West? And Ray Gebauer of Mannatech after 19 years?

Steven Spielberg
Do you know how many feet of film Steven Spielberg shot in his first big film, 'JAWS,' and, how many feet actually made the final cut?

*Over **400,000 feet of film was shot**. There was almost a mile of technical errors alone! **11,000 feet were used for the final cut.***

Less than 3% of what the master shot ended up making the grade for the final movie. Look at all the 'wrong' feet of film he and the editors had to go through to get to the 'good ones.' Think he asked: 'How many feet will I have to shoot to make a blockbuster pic?' Or 'Wonder how long this will take?'

Or do you suppose he just shot whatever it took to make the picture the way he wanted it? Even though most of it was 'mis-takes'?

The question is the answer in an interesting way. Ask the right one and you'll get what you want. Because by the question you are willing to answer, you'll get yourself to commit to doing whatever it takes to create that thing you want. And isn't that the goal? Once you're clear, there's always help available. People like helping those who are totally committed to reaching their destination. ☺

14
No more pretending you love 'no'

I have never been a glutton for unnecessary punishment. Everyone since God has talked endlessly about how to overcome, deal with, convert, or somehow take REJECTION.

Books upon books have been written whose goal is to get you to either 'reposition' or 'reframe' the dreaded 'NO' in your mind so you can stand it.

Do you remember the line "every 'no' is worth x$."?

They take an average of your sale divided by say, 10. E.g. if your sale = $100, and it takes 10 prospects before you get a 'yes,' then each 'no' is positioned as "worth $10 to you." Remember that? As nice as that sounds, especially to the consultants pushing it who have not ever sold anything themselves, this repositioning of the debilitating 'no' doesn't help most people keep going very long.

I have always believed this pain (having to endure 'no') is entirely unnecessary—and it's the #1 reason people fail in sales, including network marketing sales. Hearing the 1000 varieties of *no*, I mean.

I share the Karate Master's philosophy. In the movie, **Karate Kid**, the Karate Kid is entered into a tournament against karate students way bigger and more experienced than he is. In a panic, the 'kid' asks his Karate Master (who entered him into the tournament):

"How can I survive a direct hit (or more) by one of these black belts who are bigger and way better than I am?"

Karate Master: "Easy...No be there."

Big smile from our young hero upon picturing this delicious alternative.

I.e. LEARN TO DUCK. So you don't get hit at all.

That's the way of the new new mlmer: 'No be there' for the pukies and naysayers.

Learn to do alternative reaching out methods so you don't have to hear 'no.' Not ever. You can make the right people come to you.

And, in the rare event that some naysayer does slip in, we will show you how to say 'NO' first, a la Ms. Stud's methods (pp. 100-104).

This way, you get the first word, AND the last word. That's the way it should be. Don't you think? Aren't you the ones going first? Being entrepreneurs? This is one of the bennies. ☺

15
Stop doing things you hate in new new mlm

Doing things you really dread was the way of the old mlm.

Uhh, what things?

Well, accosting people you know every chance you get, for one. This dreaded activity is fallout from the "5th worst thing…" It's also a big reason lots of people have no place to go for Christmas dinner, or any other dinner with anyone they know.

There is no excuse for this ridiculous situation, and new new mlmers will not have it.

At speaking events I do around the country, I always ask:

"Who in the room really loves calling people you know about your products or business?"

The crowd hesitates. They become quiet and look at each other. Then, a few hands go up. (I was one of those, too, at first. I LOVED doing that.)

Of 500 people at one event, 6 raised their hands.
Of 2300 at another event, 21 raised their hands. It's pretty
much the same everywhere. Right around 1% really like
calling people they know about their business or
product/service with the intent to sell or convert.

Old and new new mlmers say, rightly, that a big reason for
people to consider mlm is the freedom it offers. Freedom
from spending most of their waking hours at jobs they hate,
getting up at dawn every day to do it, putting on pantyhose
and high heels, or starched shirts and ties, and having to
play politics, kiss up, deal with stupid bosses, etc. etc.

So then, why insist on forcing every new recruit to do the
one thing nearly all of them say they really dread?
What kind of freedom is that?

But sponsors just keep saying, "Get over it. Do it. Don't
you really believe in this thing?"   And so, new people try
it, unprepared, and get you know who on the phone, and
then, no one hears from them again. Another statistic.

Did you know that not wanting to call people (to pitch
things), especially to one's friends, is so common it has
been given names by psychologists?

"Call reluctance", "shyness" "phone terror," etc.

So here's for all new new mlmers: This is NOT something anyone needs to get over. It's OK. People can be successful in network marketing without ever calling anyone they know, or ever calling anyone first. That is the way of the new new mlmer.

Consider alternatives to make the right prospects come to you. Then **you** interview **them**. Because they called YOU. A very different approach. A very different feeling. Ask anyone who's tried it. All you need for that first call are the doctor questions (pp. 90-93).

So if you or your people aren't ready to make that first move, let the friends and family come to you. It's FINE. And works with much less stress. Because no one even HEARS no! They only hear from potential 'right ones.' Isn't that the idea?

The Truth book has 14 methods of reaching out. Most do not require calling people you know, first. Each method has made someone a millionaire. There are many ways to do this. ☺

Doing things you really dread was the way of the old mlm. ☹ Old mlm, ok? ☺

16
To use or not to use the 'mlm' word?

If they say: Is this mlm? Or network marketing? Is this a pyramid?

You can say: Well, let me tell you what we do, and you can call it whatever you want, ok? OR: Only if you're really good...(see pp. 80-81 for these two complete routines).

Some people asked if this redirection was not tantamount to 'hiding' or 'concealing' that it's mlm. They asked:

Can't we just say "Yes, it's mlm and I'm proud of it?" Or, "Well it is mlm but it's not what you think..." or "Well it's not a pyramid, really..." or "Your company's a pyramid, too." Etc.

Well, I never said or taught anything other than the two routines above after the first few months of doing the business, because:

1. I ended up spending hours with people over the definition of mlm, pyramids, etc. And mostly, the people 'arguing' had NO experience of their own. It was hearsay from others, and often, those people had just heard about someone else with a garage full of stuff.

2. I discovered after hundreds of hours of conversations of this sort, that the perceptions these people had of 'mlm' did not represent even slightly how I was practicing the business. So I decided on a new response set, to avoid bringing up in their minds perceptions that did not represent the way I practiced.

So when people asked: Is it a pyramid? MLM? Network marketing?

The standard answer was (and still is for all my students) the same:

"Let me tell you what we do and you can call it whatever you want, ok?" [see pp. 80-81 for the whole routine]

I found this question cracks open people's minds momentarily, so we could tell them what we actually did (per the script on pp. 80-81). They then responded to THAT, not to their previous perception, which I never got into anymore.

Here's how countless people responded to our answer after they gave us permission to tell:

"Oh, great. I think I could do that! For a minute I thought it was one of those things."

Amazing. That response from prospects made this clear: whatever they thought 'mlm' was, that they didn't like, it was not what my team was practicing, nor what new new mlmers practice. So we stopped discussing their definitions, and slipped in ours in this manner.

Why spend time arguing about someone's perception of a word when their definition is probably not the thing you do as new new mlmers anyway? Remember, do you want to make it in your lifetime?

Maybe the title of this little book will help. ☺

P.S. They're probably thinking of the horrors of the old mlm, anyway.☹

17
The art of network conversation-1
How do I know the product will work?

You're heavy into it. Suddenly, they ask:

"How do I know it'll work for me?"

OK. Remember the mission: Find people for whom it's the right thing to be doing now. No one else. No more recruiting anyone you have to drag across the finish line.

That said, let's pretend for this conversation that you love the product/service (because you've had results). Doesn't matter about your income for this tip to work. So, right while you're discussing away about the product:

THEM: How do I know it'll work for me?

(New new) YOU: I **don't** know, for sure. But what if it **does** work? What if it works for you the way it's worked for me? Then what? Would you want to try it then?

THEM: Uh, I don't know...

(New new) YOU: Well then this probably isn't something for you. If you won't try it even if it **will** work for you, then this is definitely not something for you. So listen, I've got another call, and I'll talk to you later, OK? Have a good one! Bye!

You need never hype anybody and predict that the product or business will work for them. After all, who knows for sure? There are so many variables unknown to you! (Like do they take it religiously? Do they have OTHER physical limitations or substance problems? Or do they believe or not believe the thing will work? Belief about what will work plays a VERY big role.)   That's why, just pose that question and await their reply.

After all, do you want this in your lifetime?   Or do you want to spend your time dragging people across the finish line? OK then, keep rolling. Have a big 'later' list. In case.

What if they say 'yes'?

THEM: Well, maybe I'd like to try it then. If it might work, I mean. So how much is it?

(New new) YOU: Well let me tell you how it comes. You get blah blah blah, and they let you have it for $/mo. Cool huh? That's why everybody buys it. So what/which one would you like to do?

THEM: (whatever...)

18
The art of network conversation-2
"How do I know the business will work?"

You're talking about the business building part. Suddenly, they ask:

"How do I know this business will work for me?"

OK. Remember the mission: Find people for whom it's the right thing to be doing. No one else. No more recruiting anyone you have to drag across the finish line.

That said, let's pretend for this conversation that you love the product/service (because you've had results). And, that either you have had some income success, or someone you know has. So, right while you're discussing the benefits of working the business:

THEM: How do I know I'll make money?

(New new) YOU: I **don't** know, for sure. But what if it does work? What if it works for you the way it's worked for me? or for [others in our company]? Or for [my aunt X]? Then what? Would you want to try it then?

THEM: Uh, I don't know...

(New new) YOU: Well then this probably isn't something for you. If you won't try it even if it **would** work for you, then this is definitely not something for you. So listen, I've got another call, and I'll talk to you later, ok? Have a good one! Bye!

You need never hype anybody and predict that business will work for them. After all, who knows for sure? There are so many variables unknown to you! (Like will they learn reaching out methods? Will they do 3-5 at all times? Will they do it in teams? Do they believe in the possibility that they can do this? Belief about what will work plays a VERY big role in the success of the thing being tried, etc.)

Just pose that question above and wait for the response.

Ask yourself: If someone stalls out when you ask them the 'what if it does work?™' question, do you think they're ready to make a change or not right now? Think they're likely to be one of the 'magic 1-4' now?

Here's what it's all about: Do you want this in your lifetime, or not?

Or do you want to keep spending your time dragging people across the finish line? What if you keep a big *later* list? In case? For now, don't you just want the 'magic 1-4'?

19
The art of network conversation-3
"Well I'd like to try the business.
So what do I do?"

If, during your conversation, your prospect says:

THEM: Well, maybe I'd like to try the business. So what would I have to do?

(New new) YOU: OK, here's what we do: We reach out in lots of ways to find people who'd like to get the same kinds of benefits we get. That's what we do to grow our business. You got that part, right?

THEM: OK, but like what? I'm not sure people I know are really the right ones...

YOU: No problem. There are lots of ways to reach out to people...whether you know them or not. For example, there are ways that make 'em come to you, and ways where you go first. Ways that cost money and ways that don't.

So you tell me which ones you want to see first, and I'll show you what we do. Then, whatever you want to try, you can watch a team that's doing that thing, either in person or over the phone. And after you watch other people doing it, you can try it. Think you could do that?

THEM: Sure.

Then you make a phone or personal date right on the spot to review the methods of reaching out that are spelled out in say, the Truth book and acted out on the Giant Heap tapes. Go through the methods sections together, so the new person can see all the choices there are. They can pick any 3-5 they feel comfortable trying.

20
The art of network conversation-4
"Should I send them a package? Costs $!"

Since info packages cost money and trees, how can you decide, when you're on the phone with someone, whether they really want a package, or they're just saying that to get you off the phone?

 We've used this with great success.

THEM: Do you have info you can send me?

YOU. Sure, but here's the deal. I'll send you the info package, if you promise you'll review it within 24 hours of the time you receive it. Then we can decide if there's a match or not. You know, save a tree. Deal?"

If you get the dreaded, "Well I don't think I can now" or "I don't know when, actually" here's you:

YOU: OK, so then, when should I send it so you could review it within 24 hours of the time you get it? So we can see if there's a match or not--you know, between what you might be looking for and what we've got. We'll save a tree till you're ready, right?

THEM: (Give you a date, or fade.)

Do not send packages unless you get this commitment. No
need to waste postage and trees. Just find out WHEN they
can review the info. If they're a real 'right one', they'll
give you a date. If they're just playing, you'll discover that
right then. BEFORE you spend your time and money on
mailings.

Save yourself for someone more ready to make a change.
Remember you don't need that many good ones to make it.
[see the Magic 1-4 pp. 34-37]

21
The art of network conversation-5
"What about flakey do-nothing downline?"

This miserable condition is a thorn in the side of anyone who has ever done network marketing. VERY anxiety producing, because they represent income you needed next week that has just gone south. Ouch!

To avoid making yourself hot or cold about these people, especially when they are just plain avoiding you, here's what you can do to feel better, and, maybe even pull a good one out of it.

Leave them a 'Goodbye Message.' You go right ahead and say 'no' first, even to these guys.

Here's a sample message to leave on their answering 'machines:'

"Hey you know Joe, it's been great leaving you these messages, but I get the feeling this just isn't the right time for you to be doing this business with us...but listen, no hard feelings. I don't want to keep bugging you about this, so, I'm not going to call you any more.

You give me a call when you're ready to make that change we talked about. You remember, blah blah blah [say the *specific thing* that attracted him in the first place]. I'll be right here. My number's 000-000-0000. Bye!"

And don't call them again until they call you.

The ones for whom it's right, now, will call you back. Those for whom it's not, now, won't. Keep seeking. Not dragging. Not begging.

22
The art of network conversation-6
"My good prospect is stalling. What can I do?"

If you can get no commitment, just hemming and hawing from someone you really want, here's a question you can ask that will get good (and busy) people off that proverbial pot:

THEM: Well, I just don't know when I could, uh…

YOU: OK. Well, let me ask you: What has to happen for you to make a decision?

Listen. Then, let go if you have to, for now. Or do whatever the person says needs to be done, whether it's wait for 2 weeks, or send info, whatever. If it's "please send info" ask for the 24-hour commitment first. (pp. 74-75)

If you don't ask for it, and just send it, you'll put yourself into that horrid mode of dialing each week and asking: "Have you reviewed it yet? (Whine) Why not? When are you going to?" Hurts just thinking about it. Ugh. ☹

A good prospect is ALWAYS a good prospect (see p. 45 for definition of a good prospect). For good people, timing is the variable you cannot control. Go ahead and ask the "…what has to happen…?" question. Then stay in touch without begging. Send info when they're ready to check it out. They'll appreciate that.

Remember, who makes up their mind? Do you? Or do they? Sigh. ☹

23
The art of network conversation-7
"What if they ask: Is this a pyramid? MLM?"

This is a biggie. Your response depends on the attitude you perceive in the voice of the questioner. If it's inquiring, NOT sneery or mean sounding, here are two good ones we've used:

Type 1 response

THEM: Is this a pyramid? Is this mlm? One of those thingies?

YOU: Well, let me tell you what we do, and you can call it whatever you want, ok?

THEM: Fair enough.

YOU: We sell [neat stuff] directly to consumers, you know, people like you and me, and we set people up in business to do the same thing. That's how the company we rep expands, and that's why they pay us. You think you could do something like that? If we showed you how?

THEM: Yeah, maybe I could. For a minute I thought it might be one of those scams--☺

Type 2 response

THEM: Is this a pyramid? Is this mlm? One of those thingies?

YOU: Only if you're really good. Otherwise, they won't let you do it. They make you start with direct sales. You know, where you sell the product to others after you love it. Then if you're really good at that, they let you start making money off the teams.

(IF) THEM: So what do you do, exactly?

YOU: Give Type 1 response above.

If they ask more specifically HOW the business is done, use the script on pp. 72-73—"what if they say 'yes'?"

See "To use or not to use the 'mlm' word" pp. 65-67 on the 'why' for these scripts versus others one might use.

24
Narrow the focus, get more attention
What an airline did

Getting people's attention. Isn't this the challenge of
everyone who's living and breathing? Young and old
alike? Here's what an airline did to get it. Attention, I
mean.

On every flight, every airline, all airline personnel are
trained to show passengers how to prepare for any
emergencies. Flight attendants are trained to do
everything they can to get EVERYONE's attention
during this important spiel.

So dutifully, on every flight, over the microphone, they go
something like:

"Ladies and gentlemen, may we have your attention please
while we show you the important safety features of this
aircraft. Blah blah blah."

If you've ever looked around, most people don't even look
up. They keep reading, listening to their headsets or
working on their laptops. Turning up the volume on the
airline speaker system has zero effect.

So one day, an enterprising attendant on Southwest
Airlines said this:

"Ladies and gentlemen: We have just found a black wallet in the front of the plane. Would you please check and see if you lost yours…"

Within seconds, everyone was feeling in their pockets, groping through their backpacks, their bags, looking in the overhead bins and generally very actively looking around, buzzing, etc.

Seeing this activity, the attendant smiled and said:

"Now that we have your attention, we'd like to explain the important safely features of this aircraft."

Everyone laughed. And paid attention.

Afterwards, some people reported that they didn't even HAVE a wallet. Yet, they were looking and feeling around anyway. Couldn't help themselves they said. What if, uh, well, who knows?

Notice the narrow focus: There was only ONE wallet. 200 people. EVERYONE looked. Because it was somehow important now. After all, what if it might affect them?

The more specific, narrow and interesting, the more people sit up and pay attention. Even those who didn't have a wallet "couldn't help themselves."

25
Cher's advice for anyone you're dragging

Hasn't everyone gotten the ones who SAY 'YES' and DO 'NO'? Or the ones who signed up, then flaked, after promising you the moon?

Well you're not the only one with those problems. Here's what Cher says to do with people who don't perform as promised.

From her #1 song in 1999 in the U.S., "Do You Believe?".

"No matter how hard I try, you keep pushing me aside...and I can't break through--there's no talking to you.

...What am I supposed to do? Sit around and wait for you?

...Well, I can't do that--there's no turning back...

...I've had time to think it through--maybe I'm too good for you...

...I can feel something inside me say, I really don't think you're strong enough...

...I don't need you anymore..."

Anyone else for 'Say *no* first'?

26
How to tell if the advice is any good or not

Before you decide what weight to give any advice you get from anyone about *anything* you're considering or doing, including the pros and cons of network marketing, do this:

After they say whatever they say to you about it, good, bad or indifferent, when they've finished, ask just one question. Do not change one syllable:

"Uh huh. Ok. So, how do you know this?"

Then be quiet and listen.

Wouldn't you want to know the basis of the advice you just received, so you can decide how much weight, if any, to give it?

When you hear what their comments, or opinions are based on, THEN you can decide on how you will let their comments influence you. ☺

This one question will help you evaluate ALL advice you receive in any area of your life. Get used to asking it, and you will see why the following two quotes have been so popular over the years:

Quote 1

"Blessed are they who have nothing to say and cannot be persuaded to say it." ☺

James Russell Lowell

Quote 2:

Napoleon Hill, after over 20 years of walking and talking with the most successful self-made leaders of our industrial age, like John Rockefeller, Andrew Carnegie, Wm. Hertz and almost 500 others, drew this conclusion about people who didn't make it financially:

"The majority of people who fail to accumulate money sufficient for their needs are...easily influenced by the opinions of others..."

Napoleon Hill, Think and Grow Rich, p. 140-141.

P.S. Before you give advice, be prepared to answer that question as well. The 'how do you know?' question. ☺

27
How to tell if your pitch is any good or not

One of the biggest challenges in running ads, card decks, ANY print medium (including the Internet) is this: how to stop pulling these loser types who end up doing nothing, or just whining. They come in with all this big talk, and then, nothing. ☹

The 'pitch' you use, i.e. the marketing message, is what will pull. You will get whom you ask for. And that can hurt. ☹

Every ad asks for something. Here are some we pulled out of major newspapers across the U.S.

Dream Opportunity!
We do 100% of the work. No meetings! No quotas! No phone calls! Make big money! Call 800.000.0000.

Turn $100 into $1,000,000 in 12 months! Amazing! Easy to accomplish! Brand New! This program will make you rich! Sit back and wait for the money to come rolling in! And it will! Call 800.000.0000

Ads like this appear everywhere, in the USA Today on Fridays, and in newspapers all over the country, in card decks, emails, fax blasts, etc.

These ads attract. Exactly who they ask for.

Here are two questions to ask of ANY ad/marketing message you or any of your babies ever run, and you'll know in advance whom you'll get. Take either of the two examples above. Ask these 2 questions about both ads:

1. Who is it attracting? I.e. what might people who respond to this ad expect? What will they have to do to get what's being offered in the ad? And then—

2. Is that (someone with those expectations) who you want on your team?

Compare your responses to the 2 questions for these two ads:

Overweight?
I lost 22 lbs. in 7 weeks, safely! Finally! Call me to find out how! 800.000.000

Leaders wanted.
National marketing group expanding in the [name city/region] area. Looking for someone who has owned or operated a business, or has experience in marketing, teaching, public/motivational speaking. Send resume to: P.O. Box 00/Call 800.000.00000

Go ahead and ask the two questions of these ads. What do you think? Whom will they attract? And is that whom the ad writers are seeking?

Adjust your marketing message until the message attracts the kind of person you seek. May take a few tries. Test it on yourself as well. Would YOU respond to it if you read it or received it?

A different set of rules seems to be operating in the brain when it is transmitting information than when it is set to receive information. That's why so few ads pull good people, no matter who writes the copy. Most people say they wouldn't respond to their own ad, if they saw it in the paper or online! But they didn't do these steps before publishing. So now you can protect yourself.

Test your marketing message with these two questions before you spend time and money running them anywhere.

And always ask: "Would I respond to this if I saw it?" Always assuming someone else had run it, of course.

28
The doctor is 'in'
"What should I say when they call?"

Picture someone calling you in response to a marketing message you've put out there. Perhaps an ad, a card deck card, a direct marketing letter, or an email or info on your website. What do you say so you don't lose a good prospect?

For best results, assume the role of a doctor. Remember the last visit to the doctor's office? What is the first question they ask you (after 'are you insured?')?

"What's wrong?" "Where does it hurt?" "What ails you?"

Why do you think they ask that? I mean, they could just start guessing, right? "Well, you look a little overweight, stressed, you're limping, you look wan, your eye is red, what's that spot on your nose?"

If they started all that before asking the 'first doctor question' wouldn't we all be surprised? But instead, they ask that first doctor question to get to why YOU came to see them, and get to it, fast.

This is the same. In your marketing message, whatever it was, there was presumably some specific information about the benefits of the product/service or of doing the business.

Therefore they are coming to you because they assume you have something they might want. A *fix*, e.g. more income, more energy, etc.

So, rather than start talking when they call, don't you think they expect you to ask WHY they called you? Like the doctor asks you right off, 'where does it hurt'? So you both can respond to what THEY came to YOU for?

OK. So here's that first doctor question that will help you find that out right off. Picture this:

THEM: I'm calling about [your ad/card/email whatever info you put out there].

YOU: Great! So, let me ask you, what attracted you?

That's your 'What ails you?' question. They came to you, remember? With this question, you will now discover (their) why.

THEM: (Either the product benefits, or the business benefits).

Right after their response here, use these two follow-ups to get a better picture of your 'patient':

YOU: Great. Let me ask you, have you ever done this sort of thing before? Direct sales, network marketing or owned your own business?

THEM: (whatever)

YOU: Great. So let me ask you this: What, ideally, are you looking for?

Jot down their responses. Just like the doctor.

This way, before you do speak, you can go into the 'files of your mind' where the specific info is, that the person calling you says they need. Not **all** the files in the cabinet of your mind about the business or product, but JUST the ones containing the info they ask you about. Exactly like the doctor tells you something specific for the ailment **you** tell **him** or **her** that you have.

Something specific that they pull out of their mental filing cabinet for **you**. Not all the other medical knowledge stored there. Hasn't that been your experience?

So how are you like a doctor? Because people are coming to you with something they'd like to make better. That's why they're calling. Right? Based on your marketing message, there's something they want that they don't have now. A need. An 'ailment' you can fix, maybe, if you can find out what it is, first. *From them.*

When 'patients' tell you what they want 'fixed', (after you've asked them the 'What attracted you?' question), you respond with the appropriate part of what you have to offer. The benefit of a product/service that can help their 'ailment' or the chance to make more income for whatever reason they want to have it.

You wouldn't want a doctor to just start treating your arm without asking, do they? Especially if it's your eye **you** want fixed. So ask.

P.S. How many times have you been to a doctor's office, and without you asking, the doctor just starts telling you where they went to medical school, why that was the best school in the history of the world, how the people who own it/run it are just the best, and why you should be so happy about that. Hmmm?

Didn't you visit the doctor because you assume all that stuff is ok? This is the same if your marketing message is specific enough and classy enough. ☺

29
How to drastically improve your odds

Do 3-5 Reaching Out Methods (ROMs, see below) well and at all times. Teach your new recruits the same.

Why 3-5? There's no guarantee which one will produce when, that's why. If you keep three balls in the air regularly, you increase your chances of finding a right one before getting depressed and giving up. Same with your babies.

How often have you heard about someone who just got started, then, the next week, you hear them say "You know, I talked to this person I know at work, and they said these things never work. I don't think I want to do this anymore."

Or, "I ran an ad, and didn't get anybody. This doesn't work." If you set your new people up to do 3-5 ROMs at all times, you won't hear those disheartening words as often. Think mutual funds. Lots of stocks in case a few don't go as planned. This too, is a place where hedging your bets is a good thing.

Commercial: For example, flipping through the Truth book, 14 ROMs are laid out in enough detail for anyone to do and do well. Take the 'Dear Friend Letter' p.86. If you and your team do that (see 'lick 'n stick party' p. 93 of the Truth), you'd have 1000 DFLs or more going out on one day. With perhaps 10-60 people calling you and yours the next week. That's just one of your ROMs.

If you then pick 'Calling lists' in teams (p. 95) and 'Streetwalking' (p. 136), that would be 3 ROMs. You can throw in say, 'Unemployment Offices' (p. 138) or 'Card Decks' (p. 128) for good measure.

Other people combine 'Newspaper Ads' (p. 105) Streetwalking and DFLs. Cruise through all the ROMs (p. 85-148) and see which ones you're most attracted to. Have your new recruits do the same.

Check http://www.mlm911.com for 'How to market on the Internet.'

End commercial. ☺

30
Reducing the effect of the dud factor

One of the least loved recommendations we (and others) have made is to do all reaching out methods (ROMs) in teams.

"Why?" some whine. "How do we know if the new guys'll be any good? It's a lot of work to schedule, and then to spend all that time with new recruits, and we don't even know if they're going to stick. I need to be recruiting new people in case these flake! What if they're duds? Ya da ya da ya da." ☹

So, you think you alone live in Dudsville? Welcome to the club.

Remember this: Every dud knows a stud. Whether they know it or not. ☺

Did you know that there are 7 (SEVEN!) duds between superstars Randy and Melissa Davis (Excel million dollar-a-year producers) and #8 down (from them)? So who's this #8? The guy who, with his organization under him, earns the Davis' nearly half of their $1 million per year. 8 deep! That's a good reason to keep all afloat, wouldn't you say?

What did the Davis' do? They just kept their duds going until... ☺

No one says you have to live with all your new signups (although Jesus did that, just about, for the 12 he picked, including one giant fake-out!). But if you want to help guarantee that they stick around long enough to bump into the likes of that #8, you must schedule reaching out activities in teams to prevent fallout.

Teams help ensure new recruits don't melt down when they hear 'No' or worse. Hearing a 'no' all alone is the beginning of the end for most new recruits. Totally unnecessary. Why do you think the expert climbers trekking up Mt. Everest are all tied together with rope?

Instead, put 2-10 team members together at a time to do calling-lists, run ads, street walk, visit unemployment offices, go mall cruising, write Dear Friend Letters, etc.

Even if some of your own front line are not the greatest, it's not really about them, but about who they know or can get to know through the ROMs. Isn't it? Do you want them all to last until #8, or not? There will be no #8 if you cannot keep 1-7 together. Ergo the reaching out teams.

If you will keep hopeful and optimistic people together for this most perilous part of the business, you will help ensure they stay in a little longer. Long enough until they or one of theirs runs into a good one. Think #8.

31
The goodbye message

How often have you spoken to prospects a few times, they seemed interested, and then, all of a sudden, they don't call back anymore? All you get is their answering machine. You've sent them the info pack, perhaps they've even been to a meeting or participated in a conference call. Now, suddenly, nothing.

It hurts. It's infuriating. Worse, deep inside, it's humiliating because you've worked on them, had high hopes for them, maybe told others about them, and probably thought you needed them desperately. And didn't they say they needed it, too? The extra income, I mean?

So now what?

Well, how about a pre-emptive strike? Say 'no' first. Yes. To your wishy washy prospects. How? Get really good at leaving them a 'good-bye message', especially on their answering machine. You'll be amazed at what happens.

Remember your mission: Find people for whom it's the right thing to be doing now...whether it's joining your business or trying the product or service.

Remember what that means: No more recruiting anyone you have to drag across the finish line.

All right then. Call them one last time and say the following words with gentleness, kindness, warmth and tenderness ☺:

"Hello, Joe? Listen, this is Mae West. From X (company name). I've left you a couple of messages, but this one's the last one. I won't be calling you anymore because I don't want to be a bug.

BUT, whenever you're ready to [*move out of your car into an apartment, whatever they told you they wanted when you asked them 'the doctor question'], you let me know. I'll be here. It's just that I'm on a deadline right now. I have to find people who want what they want RIGHT NOW.

So, whenever you're ready to get that thing you told me you want, call. I'll be right here, OK? My number's XXX-XXXX. OK? Talk to you later. Bye!"

Watch what happens. The ones who really seek to change their lives now will call you pronto. Those for whom the timing is not right, for ANY reason, will not. But, isn't that all you want? To find the ones for whom it's the right thing to be doing? And to find them in your lifetime? Without dragging? Aren't you looking for the magic 1-4s?

32
Say 'no' first

Based on the drop out rates of 90%+ over the last 60 years, it's obvious that the most difficult part of the mission:

'Find people for whom it's the right thing to be doing now…'

is to survive the process of sharing, telling and converting at all.

You know the doubters, yes? Anyone who is not ready to hear about anything new and different right now, and who starts dumping on you and it before they know anything about it.

Well, perhaps the best, and most surprising defense for this is to go on the offense: say 'no' first. There are lots of ways to do it, depending on your mood, how prickly they are to you, and their relationship to you.

Anyone who's spent even one week in the trenches doing the business knows that of the wrong ones, a small set are really mean, sneery and just kind of pukey-like.

For some reason, the biggest pukey types are friends, family and neighbors. So, depending on your spunk, here are some tested and fun responses you can give when they make those yucky comments to you.

The following responses are designed to keep your fragile ego whole, so you can keep on keeping on for another day, as many days as it takes to get those 'magical 1-4' somewhere in your organization.

The STANDARD SAY 'NO' FIRST routine is the following, spoken in an almost apologetic manner. Use it whenever you hear the negative stuff coming on:

> YOU: You know, uh, I think you're right. This is probably not something for you. At least not now. Listen I have another call. Gotta go. Have a good one, ok? Bye! ☺

The following are variations, and fun responses to specific zingers that networkers hear from their friends, family and neighbors.

THEM: So what do you know about [getting rich, healthy, etc.] ☹

> YOU: You're right. I don't know much about getting rich yet, but I've got some new friends who do know and I'm going to learn from them. I don't think it's for you though, at least not now. See you later. Got another call. Bye! ☺

THEM: Your own business? They took you for a sucker, that's for sure. Can't you get a real job? What's wrong with you? ☹

YOU: You know, Uncle Donald, I made a mistake calling you. There's this lady who's very successful---and she said there'd be pukey types who'd dump on this without knowing anything about it. I didn't think it would be you, though...OK. Talk to you later, Uncle Donald. Bye! ☺

THEM: Uhh, I don't know. Is it one of those things? Would I have to spend my own money? How much would you make on me? ☹

YOU: You know Mary, you're right. I'm talking about starting a business of your own. I don't think it's something you could do, though. Because you'll have to put out something. Some time, some money maybe, some good energy and some imagination. But I don't think this is for you. It's OK. You stay the way you are. Gotta go. Bye! ☺

More? OK.

THEM: It's too expensive! ☹

YOU: You're right. It is too expensive for you, really out of your league. It's OK though. This is not something for you. Got another call. Talk to you later. Bye! ☺

THEM: I don't have any time or money and anyway...☹

> YOU: Well, I can certainly see why. Actually, you're right. If you think you can't , you're right. Henry Ford said that, did you know that? Gotta go–another call! ☺

THEM: I don't have any time or money and anyway...☹

> YOU: OK. Well you let me know when you're ready to make a change in either of those areas, OK? Gotta go—another call. Talk to you later! Bye!☺

THEM: Well, I'm not sure. Like I said last time, it sounds interesting, but I'm pretty busy. Maybe later...☹

> YOU: Well, we've already talked a few times, let's do this: you let me know when you're ready to make that change we talked about and DO something about it. I don't want to be a bug, so you let me know when you're ready. I won't call you again. I love ya still, but I'm on a deadline. I need people who are ready to do something NOW. I'll be here for you whenever, OK? Gotta go. Another call. Bye! ☺

Sound too fast? Remember you can keep a *later* list going. But for now, don't you want to find your magic 1-4?

104

And do you want that in your lifetime? Or do you really prefer dragging?

You can ALWAYS come back to ANYONE later, AFTER you have some right people first. You can always set up a charity for some of them after you've made it…☺

33
Quick way to 'web-ify' yourself'

How can you get your daily dose of Web news and info without spending half the day trying to find it?

One way: Create a personalized news page on Yahoo! or Excite.

Both portals let you customize the day's headlines to get plenty of news about the Internet and news in any area of interest you have. If you want to track a specific publicly traded company, you can add its stock ticker to your page. Click on the symbol, and you'll receive quotes and links to stories. Then make it a 'favorite', or even have that be your start-up page when you log on, and you'll get it all on one customized-for-you page.

For setting up a personalized Yahoo! Page, go to http:///www.yahoo.com and click on "My" at the top of the page, and for Excite, go to http://www.excite.com and click on 'New Members'.

Sign up on top of the page.

Wonderful. Time saving. I have a 'my Yahoo' page.

(Info from Fast Company magazine, Jan-Feb issue, 2000)

34

"The Internet is the greatest Direct Marketing medium ever invented"

So says Seth Godin, author of 'Permission Marketing' and VP of Direct Sales at Yahoo!

While few would argue with that, most people and websites on the net are not making a dime yet. 98% are in the hole. A big hole.

How many people do you know, personally, who have taken the time and money to set up their websites, then sit back and fervently hope and pray that they'll attract visitors and maybe even sell something?

Then after mom and dad, nobody else comes. Nobody told them they'd have to 'market' their website. Oops!

According to Godin, who specializes in direct marketing online, there were some 50 million visitors surfing the web everyday in 1999. That sounds like a lot, right? However, there were 2 million (!!) corporate and mom & pop Web sites up and running in 1999 (when he was writing his book).

That means on average, there are 25 people per web site per day. Kind of like having 8 million TV networks instead of just 10 for you to choose from every night. Picture it. Think of the remote control you'd need (!).

Godin says it's costing all those companies (including lots of home based business people) about US$1 billion to create, maintain and update their websites. Easy to see why almost nobody's making any money. Not with just 25 visitors available, on average, per day, for each website.

You can guess the Internet stats, yes? Less than 1% of the websites get nearly ALL the traffic.

Yahoo! and America Online, each grab millions of those precious visitors every single day. How can **you** make money on the Internet, then, with your measly 100 hits a month?

Find people for whom your business/product is the right thing to be doing and taking/using. No one else. Remember that?

Here's how, on the Internet, to MAKE THE RIGHT ONES OF THEM COME TO YOU. ☺

35
Target the right customers online

Patricia Seybold, author of the Wall Street Journal best seller 'Customers.com' says that of the '8 Critical Success Factors' for marketing online, #1 is:

"Target the Right Customers"

If she has to tell corporate marketing chiefs across the US to target the right customers, you can bet you're not the only one who's been getting the wrong people, or no one at all. Lots of people, in all kinds of businesses, have been getting pathetic results. People whose companies spend a lot more than you do on marketing on the Internet (and everywhere else).

She writes that the percentage of 'right ones' FOR ANYONE'S business is a tiny fraction of the total people out there. Of course, you know this now. And like for us, because the total numbers 'out there' are so big, if even just 1% of say, 5 million people, buy your product or service, that gives almost anyone enough income to be more than comfortable.

Figure it out. How much would you take in if 50,000 people (1% of 5 mil) spent just $10 on your stuff?

The trick: finding people who want what you have.

36
Finding people online who want what you have

These are the ones for whom it's the right thing to be doing now, no one else. Remember?

So how do you get mostly right ones online, by 'targeting your market'? One way: email. And you need not, and should not, spam tens of thousands of people who have no interest and will report you to the spam police.

Use quality opt-in mailing lists instead.

These are lists of people who have ASKED to receive information on a specific topic, e.g. entertainment, sports, health, alternative health, marketing on the internet, pets, home based business, mlm/networking, soccer moms, etc. There's an opt-in email list for almost any topic you can imagine. Thousands of them.

Each person on these lists has opted-in, i.e. ASKED to be on the list to receive free, and presumably relevant, timely and interesting information about that topic. They're there to be educated and to exchange information. Of course, if people like the info in the emails that they receive, they may order whatever. AFTER seeing that what is offered is helpful or interesting. A sales letter is not usually helpful or interesting to anyone but the writer. You need to offer something of value, interest, or fun **to the reader first.**

See pp. 120-126, for example. Or go to
http://www.myharvardeditor.com for guidelines and private
consultations.

There are thousands of opt-in email lists, some with tens of
thousands of subscribers.

Anyone can sign up for these lists. Usually for free. The
names on these lists are available for rent to people who
want to reach certain groups with their message. You can
do this, and target your potential audience.

Cost to rent these names? Typically .20-.25 per name,
depending on how many you rent for an emailing campaign
(or just for a test marketing emailing).

There's usually a minimum order of US$100-200.

BONUS: Those who respond to your email message
become part of YOUR private opt-in list and you don't pay
for them if you email them again. Cool huh?

Now, where do you find these lists? Check out these
websites (there are more, but this will get you going):

http://www.liszt.com
http://www.imediafax.com
http://www.edmarketing.com
http://signup.postmasterdirect.com

P.S. Imediafax has an incredible 'media fax' distribution service. Great for those of you who've always wondered how to get yourself interviewed on radio or TV, or how to get someone to write a story about your product or service in the paper. An editorial, rather than an ad. Editorial comments outpull a typical ad about 3,000 to 1.

37
How to create effective email messages, with permission

Marketers have said that the biggest problem for ANYONE using email to market on the Internet is this: almost no one believes anything they read anymore, unless it's from people or brands they know and trust.

So many email messages offer the moon, for little or no work, effort or money, that good prospects just turn off their brains, and hit 'delete'.

Spam (unsolicited) messages are usually the worst, because they're both an unexpected intrusion AND totally unbelievable and full of hype. Even messages to opt-in list members are sometimes ridiculous, as everyone discovers when they sign up for them. So you'll see how not to, at least.

If you have a good business opportunity or top quality products or services, here's how to send an email message:

1) send it to people who are open to receiving info about what interests or concerns you might have in common, and

2) write it in a way that makes it intriguing to the recipient so they don't hit 'delete'

First dictate of effective email marketing:

Create a series of messages, like episodes in a TV series (think 'Sopranos'), each one getting into it a little more. Each successive one with a little surprise or unexpected twist.

Why a series? Effective email marketing is like dating. Getting to know each other takes more than one date, does it not? Who really wants to be thought of as a one-email stand?

No one wants to think they're that easy. And if they are, how good do you think they'll be? How long will they last? Easy come easy go.

The little voices

When you or anyone else receives an email, what do the little voices in the brain whisper as you read it?

What's this about? Oh, OK. Do I care about this or not? Yeah. But can I believe/trust this? Do they sound real? Do they really know anything or are they just trying to sell me something? Oh, looks like maybe they do have something I'd like to see...hmmm. Well let me look (click)

If this happens when people read your first message, you've just scored big: you've gotten the best you could hope for on your first email date: their ATTENTION. Just like that first look, and then, smile. Great start! Now, they'd like to go to the next step and see more. What should that be? So you don't lose them now?

Go first class. Send friendly, conversational, informative, non-cluttered looking messages. Read your own message and pretend you received it from someone. Would you respond or not? Rework it until you'd respond to your own message. Not easy. Not fast. Sorry. Want immediate help? Go to http://www.harvardeditor.com, run by Ms. Stud.

Know what NOT to send anyone, ever. For example, here's a guaranteed delete from anyone with brains:

Does the thought of making up to $208,000.00 in the next six months appeal to you?

*** If you're looking for a perfect part-time business, with little work required... then this one's for you!

*** If you're operating with very little start-up capital, yet you want to make up to $200,000.000 OR MORE per year... then this powerful program is really for you!!

*** If you've recently lost all your money, and you need to start a business that will support you for life... then this AMAZING program is definitely for you!!! Blah blah blah...!!!

Who do you think this message attracts? With words like
'little work required' and offering that kind of income?

Uh huh. And is that who you want on your team?

(Lots more examples of how NOT TO on our website:
http://www.maxout.com/email.htm)

Do you really want anyone you can get?

P.S. Remember whom Mr. Godin says you'll get with
messages like those above ☹:

They will *"attract the dreaded 'Opportunity Seekers'...that
someone with more time than money, a nonconsumer who
focuses on low-margin items and is a less than ideal
prospect for most products....lower income..." ibid. p 109*

OK. Enough said. ☺

38
Romancing your prospects

Lest you think you're the only one that can't find any
really right ones to romance...

Every struggling Networker in every corner of the world
wonders several times a day where those people are, who
are going to make them rich, famous and able to at least
semi-retire. I hear from lots of them. And why not? Isn't
that the idea? Isn't that prospect the biggest reason to
endure this often painful and anxiety producing process?
Until one or two of those wonderful people are unearthed?

So where are they, anyway? Well, you'll be interested to
know that you're not the only ones with that challenge (to
put it mildly).

Fortune 500 companies have had the same problem for
decades. And they spend a lot more marketing money than
you do. Even with their huge marketing budgets, where to
find the people who are right for their service or product
eludes many of them. And then, once they get them, how to
keep them from switching. Arghhhh! How often has
someone you know switched, say, phone companies
for a mere $30?

EVERY marketing chief of EVERY company starts off believing his/her product or service is the best and should be bought by just everyone. Sounds just like well, you know.

But for some reason that no one at McDonald's has ever been able to figure out, everyone in the world does NOT eat there. Nor can anyone explain to General Motors why every one does not buy a Chevy, or some other GM car. Same problem at Honda, and for Celine Dion, the Backstreet Boys or Victoria's Secret. Do they wish everyone loved them? But does everyone? And does everyone buy them?

So does that mean they're not good?

Think even Jesus, or Buddha, or Gandhi, or Mohammed, or, well, Crest toothpaste. Does everyone love them?

So then, the marketers and supporters go from wishing they could have a total monopoly on the market (i.e. 100% of everybody) to settling for a tiny percent of the whole market out there. They call it market share.

Like .5% or 1 or 2% of the market out there. Even that is VERY expensive to find and keep. But valuable enough, as we saw before. Small percents of huge numbers return enough money to keep marketers chasing them full time.

And working on keeping them.

And on the Internet, it's way bigger. With some **75 million people now reported to be surfing the web daily**, how does anyone get the attention of ANYONE? That's just ATTENTION! Having someone's attention doesn't mean a sale, yet. Just getting attention is a VERY BIG THING. (That's why companies spent $2-3 million dollars (US) for ONE 30-second spot in the Superbowl of 2000. Just for the time slot. The Census Bureau crowed about their 'bargain' of $1.6 mil for their 30-second spot!)

Bigger than attention itself is getting the attention of those elusive 'right ones'. Remember, do you really want everyone's attention? Or just the attention of the 'right' ones? Think dragging...☹

Seth Godin from Yahoo.com shows in his Permission Marketing book why almost no one gets hits (=attention) on their websites. Including most of the big guys. Even though the big players with humungous ad budgets market their sites to 'everyone.' Miserable results so far for the large majority of them.

So now, one new, big marketing thing is this: Targeting the Audience.

Well, if this is the latest and greatest marketing focus of the big Internet companies, you can bet that they've been wasting major money and efforts chasing the wrong ones, too.

That's why they have to hire high priced consultants like Patricia Seybold and Yahoo's Seth Godin who tell them this:

> focus on the 'right' ones. ☺

Oh.

39
What should you say to your 'target' audience?

I don't mean targets to shoot at or 'get'. Rather, right ones who might share your interests or concerns or philosophies, and who might advance with you. Think farming. Not overpowering or defeating. The latter has made for short-lived partnerships, as any experienced networker can tell you first hand.

So plan on romancing your prospects. It may take a few messages. This is like dating, farming, or having a baby for those first few years. Remember the first dictate of effective email marketing? Create several messages that will be received in sequence. First date, second date, third date, etc.

For that first email overture: Be as specific, narrow and *limiting* as you can. The more precise and exclusive the focus, the more attention you will attract. Yes.

Because it's unexpected and therefore interesting.☺

Recall what one airline did to get the attention of all 200 passengers during their innovative routine 'safety features' announcement. (pp. 82-83)

OK. Example. Let's say you're in a health/nutrition company. Pretend you're in it because the product helped you reduce or end backaches you've been having for years.

Say also you're a woman. One headline you can use to attract some 'right' ones is:

> To all women who suffer from chronic back pain. Click here for 3 free tips on how I reduced the pain safely and naturally.

Would you respond to this if you had back pain and were a woman? What if you were a woman but had no back pain. Would you want to see what tips they were offering? Yes? Oh. To pass the info on to someone you know who IS suffering? Me too.

Now, let's say you're a blonde. We'll stretch it more.

> To all blonde women who suffer from chronic back pain. Click here for 3 free tips on how to reduce the pain safely and naturally.

Wouldn't you just wonder what it might be that works especially well for blondes? What do you brunettes think when you read that? ("Well I wonder what they might have for brunettes with chronic back pain like me....hmmm")

Did this message get your attention? Would you hit delete summarily without clicking on the '3 free tips...'?

Does this focus in your message mean your company has no other products? Doesn't matter.

The headline attracts many of the 'right' people. Those you've specified right in your header, and perhaps those who thought of people while reading it who might benefit from your '3 free tips' on this specific concern. Go ahead and ask the two questions of the ads we laid out before:

Who is this attracting?   Is this whom we seek?

Tip: You can have the tips on a website for people to click on and check out, or you can have them email you or email an autoresponder which would send out those free tips automatically. Perhaps one a day.

Go to http://www.aweber.com or http://www.getresponse.com for autoresponder info and wonderful service. An autoresponder is like a fax-on-demand (fod), only on the Internet, and sends out emails instead of faxes. You must prepare the content, just like with the fods. But the autoresponder will send the emails. Unlimited. In the sequence you specify. Incredible service.

Runs about $20/mo for unlimited emailing of sequential messages. Just like the 'first dictate' of effective email marketing says. You just cook up the messages.☺

For the opening salvo, in our example, we've selected ONE benefit (the backaches). So how does one select which benefit to put?

Start with the one that means the most to you, personally. That will begin the attraction process for like-minded souls. Once they hear more over time, you can always introduce other remedies that work for different things. But isn't the point of the first 'email overture' to attract the right people and get their attention and hold it so they keep reading? And not hit 'delete'?

Think what major department stores do. Macy's has their 'White Sale' several times each year. Those headlines in every newspaper attract droves to their stores each time they run the announcement.

Now, do you really think that the shoppers, once there, shop only for linens and then leave? Think they maybe go to other departments and load up on other things they see? Things that they DID NOT COME down to Macy's to buy based on the 'White Sale' pitch??

This is the same. Interest people with something specific first. They'll see what else is there when they get there. One overture at a time. Remember this is like dating. What happens with most first overtures? Doesn't it START the process? ☺ (Or end it right then ☹).

Check out our site for constant updates on what's new that's working on the Internet for people marketing to the 'right ones.' http://www.mlm911.com. And our site, http://www.harvardeditor.com for tips on how to edit your marketing message copy so they pull 'right' ones. ☺

40
Say it with a signature

How do people get those little notes and links by their signature at the end of their emails?

For example:

Kim Klaver, AKA Ms. Stud
How to do network marketing with or without your friends, family or neighbors. Visit http://www.mlm911.com
816.333.6619

 The little piece of info underneath the name (along with the name, of course) is called a signature, or 'sig'.

A great way to tell everyone you email something about what you do. You can add an electronic signature to your emails one time, and that's it. The whole thing appears each time you send out an email

And you can have one signature for business, and a different one for family or a secret amour.

Outlook Express, for example, has a Help item when you have the program on. Click on that. Hit 'signature' in the index, and it shows you step by step how to do it. You can change them whenever you want to. Same for Netscape.

Notice I also put my website address, **including** the 'http' part. That way it's ONE click for recipients of my emails to go visit my site, or a specific page on my site. Make it easy for them to get to the site or email you. ONE CLICK.

You can do the same. Go to the page you want visitors to go to directly, and 'select' the entire top 'http' address from the top of the window. 'Copy' that, and 'paste' it into your email or into the signature. Done! And you made no mistakes because you copied it electronically.

It's also easy to enter an autoresponder email address instead of or along with a website address. If you don't have a website, but have set up an autoresponder email service, put the address. Then, when people click on that autoresponder email address, it automatically draws down the familiar email window, with the autoresponder 'to:' email address all filled in. People just have to hit 'send' and they will receive the email that you have created for just that purpose, be it #1, #3 or #7.

Of course, put a message to motivate someone to click on the email address. For example: *Click here 'mailto:email address' to receive 3 free tips on how to legally reduce your income tax through overlooked deductions.*

Easy to change the sig whenever you want.

41
For writers

A wonderful way to get the word out without 'selling' directly is to offer tips and helpful information in the form of articles or news releases. Most websites need content to drive traffic there. That's why many sites have news, stocks, etc. Some content costs, some is free. Content can be information and tips on health, youth, taxes, home based businesses, etc. There are hundreds of topics of interest.

Here's an example for people marketing skin care lines, or nutritionals that help skin look better:

> 7 free tips on how to make your skin look young again without surgery or drugs. Click here.

Tips on almost anything are interesting to most people. Especially free ones. So write them up. And make them available online. On a website, or autoresponder, where they arrive as emails.

And at the end of your piece, of course, they see a website address or your email address, or your autoresponder email address. All they do is 'click' and presto!

So how do you get your article out there on other people's websites, where strangers might read it?

There are websites that collect e-articles for e-zines. They get them 'out there' so website owners can choose what they want to post. And why do website owners seek content? So they have something there besides the goods and services they want to sell. Like one network television owner once said about TV, the 'programming is an annoyance we have to deal with to put the ads out there for our viewers.'

This is similar. Website owners have goods and services to offer. They need good content to go along with it. All you do is write the content for topics that might be related to their sites.

Not sure how to write them? Check out articles you like, and model yours on those. Here are some great sites to get you going on helping you get your pieces out there.

http://www.ezinearticles.com/add_url.htm
http://www.web-source.net/articlesub.htm
http://216.147.104.180/articles/submit.shtml
http://www.digitalwork.com/

More on editing your copy so it attracts the right ones at the http://www.harvardeditor.com site.

42
So now what?

A revolution always starts with an idea someone feels very strongly about. What lifts an idea to one that can trigger a revolution is that many others, secretly or openly, share the same strong feelings, at about the same point in historical time, independently of one another.

The bitter frustrations of which these Rules were born are shared by many around the world. It is this knowledge that has given impetus and life to this little volume. With these *Rules* I have tried to acknowledge the frustrations of so many, and offer alternatives, so that those who share these feelings can be encouraged with new, working ideas and can band together to change the old ways. Thus the new new MLMer.

The old mlm must change if the industry is to attract top talent and prevent the attrition of its current practitioners, who continue to go down in legions like Achilles, never knowing what hit them. This is not a good thing. Nor a necessary thing.

It is said a revolution begins when one person speaks their mind about certain inequities, indignities, unjust happenings, and then another, and another. One after another until there is an unstoppable moving mass, all of one mind, all mad, and all determined not to take it anymore. Best get out of its way as it rolls across the land.

In the mlm world, change also happens one person at a time. With one wonderful exception. The speed of it.

Networkers are already connected around the world with existing voicemail systems, national and regional conference calls, countless meetings around the world and now, the Internet. One click can send new information to tens of thousands who send it on to tens of thousands more.

No need to wait for Paul Revere to come riding into town with the latest news.

For all those who believe that the *New New MLM* is coming, let this little book guide you in how to be a member of the new society—a good *New New MLMer*.

Bibliography (abbreviated version)

Customers.com Patricia Seybold. 1999 Times Business
Permission Marketing. Seth Godin.1999 Simon & Schuster
The Cluetrain Manifesto Levine, et al. 1999 Perseus Books
The JAWS Log. Carl Gottlieb. 1975. Dell
The Law of Success. N. Hill. 1992 50th printing. Success
Unlimited.
The New New Thing. M Lewis. 1999 Norton&Co.
The 7 Lost Secrets. Joe Vitale. 1992 281.999.1110
Think and Grow Rich. N. Hill. 1990 Ballantine Books

Ordering *Rules for the New New MLMer*

For bulk orders and bulk pricing of this book,
call Max Out Productions 1.800.595.1956 or Sound
concepts 1.800. 544.7044.

Or visit http://www.mlm911.com or
http://www.maxout.com ☺

Also by Kim Klaver (aka *Ms Stud!)*

Audios

So, You want to be a Networker?
A single audio which gives a humorous introduction to
what it takes to make it in the networking business. 1996.

How to Build a Giant Heap
With or without your friends, family or neighbors
A 2-tape set for people in the business. 1997

How to be an Awesome Sponsor
And Keep your Heap
A single audio which shows people how to keep the ones
the want to keep. 1998

Books

The Truth...
What it really takes to make it in Network Marketing
A 200-page full color cartoon training guide with 14
reaching out methods laid out in fun detail. 1999

Websites

http://www.maxout.com or http://www.mlm911.com
http://www.newnewmlm.com
http://www.harvardeditor.com

Kim Klaver, aka *Ms Stud!*

About the Author

Harvard, Stanford and MIT educated. Author of 7 academic books. Switched to Network Marketing in pursuit of gangster money. Hit Network Marketing superstar status in 1994, setting a whole new standard for people in the industry.

Max Out Productions, Inc. was established in 1996 to help all entrepreneurs who choose Network Marketing to *survive* the process of finding the right ones, and to *enjoy* it.

As the creator of the hilarious hit audio series 'How to Build a Giant Heap with or without your friends, family or neighbors', the best selling cartoon training guide 'The Truth…What it really takes to make it in Network Marketing', and now 'Rules for the New New MLMer', Kim achieves her goal of "inspiring millions" with her unique brand of motivational entertainment.

She stands alone in the industry teaching methods and techniques; how to make people come to you, how to say 'no' first, how to get quality resumes, how to do marketing in teams, where to get the top talent and most of all, how *not* to turn off the best people.

Says Ms Stud: "Good people expect to be wooed. They don't expect to be dragged into the back seat on the first date. No. The recruiting process for good people is like gentle allure. You open the kimono just a little, then, walk away. The good ones always come back for more."

Ordering *Rules for the New New MLMer*

To order single and bulk copies of this book and the rest of the *Ms Stud!* Collection call Max Out Productions, Inc. 1.800.595.1956 or Sound concepts 1.800. 544.7044, or visit http://www.mlm911.com